"I was delighted to read an advanced copy of Amy Meekins' devotional, *Heart re-CHARGE*! Amy has a fresh voice and wonderful insight into the Scriptures she has chosen to feature in this book. Each devotion includes a key Scripture, a sincere prayer, and thought provoking questions that will help readers consider how they can apply Biblical principles to their lives. If you are looking for encouragement and new insight into Scripture, then you'll enjoy this book from a special young woman who has overcome many challenges to shine bright for Jesus."
Carrie Turansky, Pastor's Wife and Award-winning Author of Inspirational Fiction

"*Heart re-CHARGE* by Amy Meekins is such an encouraging daily devotional for all ages. Amy has a way in showing God's love toward us. In Ephesians 2:10 it states, "For we are God's masterpiece." Amy has the ability to display this in each daily devotion. I am so thankful that the Lord has spoken through Amy and how she has been able to share His unconditional love to ALL!"
Shari Falwell, Senior Pastor's wife, Thomas Road Baptist Church

"The devotions in *Heart re-CHARGE* are the outgrowth of Amy Meekins' experiences as a child and young adult living with CHARGE Syndrome. What she's come to understand about herself, about God, and her relationship with Him can bring hope to others. Her personal thoughts and the reflection activities presented in this book are a good starting place for young people seeking to find their place and purpose in the world."
Jolene Philo, co-author of *Sharing Love Abundantly in Special Needs Families: The 5 Love Languages® for Parents Raising Children with Disabilities*

"With these devotionals, Amy invites us into her personal conversations with her God as she responds to a daily Scripture reading. With disarming honesty and sincerity, she leaves the reader with a thought and a challenge. This refreshing book will encourage you in your own relationship with Him!"
Julie Zine Coleman, author of *Unexpected Love: God's Heart Revealed through Jesus' Conversations with Women* and managing editor of *Arise Daily*

"Amy Meekins is a beautiful reflection of Jesus. Her smile brightens a room and her joy is so evident to everyone who meets her. We always feel blessed after spending time with her. Amy shows us how to be strong and persevere through trials. She inspires us to focus on what is important in life. It is a delight and honor to call her friend."
Linda and Jen Barrick, HopeOutLoud.com

"*Heart re-CHARGE Devotionals* is a great devotional book to help you grow closer to God and reCHARGE your relationship with Him! Through the book, you learn a lot about Amy as she is amazingly transparent and shares some of her deepest fears and yet shares how much she loves God! I love how Amy shared a verse every day and then wrote out a prayer and followed that with a challenge for the reader to apply the verses. This is a perfect quick devotional that you can use everyday and perfect to do along with your child with special needs, especially as we are learning about Amy living life with a disability. I highly recommend this devotional book to everyone! It will help reCHARGE your life with Christ! Thank you, Amy, for sharing your heart and allowing us to see Jesus through your eyes!"
Stephen "Doc" Hunsley, M.D., Executive Director, SOAR Special Needs

Heart
re-CHARGE
Devotionals

Amy ♡ :)
Romans 12:12

Heart re-CHARGE

Devotionals

Amy Christine Meekins

Heart re-CHARGE *Devotionals*

Library of Congress Cataloging-in-Publication Data
LCCN: 2020923291
ISBN: 978-1-64775-238-5

Edited by Alisa Jacinto.

Cover design by Arnulfo Jacinto.

Interior design and artwork by Alisa and Arnulfo Jacinto.

Printed in the United States of America.

Published by
Vervante
224 South Main St STE 202
Springville, UT 84663

DEDICATION

I dedicate this book to God. He created me. He allowed me to grow and develop beyond anyone's expectations. He offered me His free gift of salvation through my Savior, Jesus Christ. He walks with me every minute of every day. To Him be the glory.

And to my family. Every single person in my family--my dad, my mom, my sister, Katie, my sister, Becca, and my brother, Josh--participated in my development. Each one of you brought something different, specific, and unique to the table. You all worked very hard in helping me to walk, and talk, and read, and play, and learn. I could not be me without you.

Table of CONTENTS

Preface

Introduction

Table of CONTENTS (continued)

PREFACE

One day I was feeling a little lonely. We were living far from town in what we called "the country house." A new friend, Jen Barrick, had written a book of prayers and her mom, Linda, gifted me with one.

I picked up the book and started reading through those prayers.

Then, I was inspired to begin writing out my own prayers. I also remembered that my dad often writes prayers to God. After a while, I decided to turn my writing into a devotional so that others could be encouraged by God's Word and what He was teaching me.

Acknowledgments

Writing a book is so much bigger than I thought it would be.

There are so many pieces. I could never do this alone. I wish to acknowledge those who have had a part in making this happen.

Alisa Jacinto - thank you for using your gift of attention to detail to edit this book. You captured the fonts and set up the format just the way I wanted them. Not only are you an amazing editor but you are a wonderful friend.

Arnulfo Jacinto - I could not have imagined having such a talented artist be available and involved to create the beauty that is the cover and the images inside these pages. You worked so hard to get every color and every design just perfect. Thank you for sharing your awesome talent and for your friendship.

Jen Barrick - I have watched you in your own ministry bless so many. That you would choose me as your friend is something very special. Thank you for sharing your story. You have been an inspiration.

And last, but not least, thank you to my lovely parents. You never give up on me. You were the ones who first gave me the idea of turning my prayer journal into a devotional. We had some great times reading every prayer multiple times and discussing how you could help me make this book into something that could encourage others. Those hours around the dining room table brainstorming on how to engage the readers and making decisions about fonts and artwork will always be a treasure to me.

INTRODUCTION

Are you wondering if God knows about you? Do you sometimes doubt His love for you?

This book is for you if:
    You are struggling.
    You are tired.
    You are mad.
    You feel as if you are being tested.
    You are sad.
    You are looking for answers.
    You are looking for Someone who cares.
    You need to know Someone understands.
    You need to know that you are not alone.
    You want to explore solutions to your questions.
    You want to find victory.
    You want to grow.

You can engage with this book in any way that blesses you.

However, here are some suggestions from me that will help you get going:

- You might want to start out with reading the Bible verse at the beginning of each chapter and taking a minute to think about it.
- Then, read the prayer under the Bible verse. You may find that you also are feeling a similar way.
- Now, you may be ready for YOUR TURN. This is the place where you make this experience YOURS. Get honest with yourself and lean on the God who made you.

What is in YOUR TURN?
    Questions.
    An invitation to journal.
    Quizzes!
    Proposals that you practice telling a Bible story.
    Suggestions to write prayers.
    Action steps you can take.
    Encouragement to sing.
    An appeal to get creative with:
        Drawing a picture,

Painting a rock,
Making a bookmark,
Grabbing a friend or a family member and doing a role play,
Making a little book,
Using sidewalk chalk,
Working with beads,
Molding something with clay.

In one YOUR TURN, you will learn how to do a demonstration to teach an important truth.

You can do this experience totally alone with God or you can invite a friend to do the book with you. Maybe you will want to use this book as a Bible study Guide for you and a group of people.

Whatever way you chose to use this book, my goal is that you know and love Jesus better in the end.

*"Do everything
without complaining and arguing,"
Philippians 2:14 (NLT)*

1

CONTENTMENT

Dear God,

Where do You want me to be? I want to belong. I want to be in a place where I fit in. Why do we live in the country so far away from my favorite places?

I know You want me to always be content with what I have and not grumble or complain about what I do not have, but sometimes I want things that are not in front of me.

God, my Heavenly Father, I do not want to do things my way. I want to do things Your Way and in Your Truth with the Life You have for me!

One of the things that is not in front of me right now is wanting to attend a school I fell in love with.

Thank You, God, for the things I DO have in front of me right now, and I pray that I can be more content.

In Jesus' name I pray,
Amen!

Do you struggle with God's will? Is there a fight within you between what God has for you right now and what you really want to happen?

Tell God your struggle. Ask Him to help you to be content.

~~~~~~~~~~~~~~~~
~~~~~~~~~~~~~~~~

"Dear brothers and sisters, when troubles of any kind come your way, consider it an opportunity for great joy. For you know that when your faith is tested, your endurance has a chance to grow. So let it grow, for when your endurance is fully developed, you will be perfect and complete, needing nothing. If you need wisdom, ask our generous God, and He will give it to you. He will not rebuke you for asking." James 1:2-5 (NLT)

2

GREAT JOY

Dear God,

Thank You for giving me joy! Thank You for enabling me to endure. From the time I was young, so many times I felt alone among my peers. I remember in middle school youth group, I tried so hard to fit in, but it just never seemed to work. Then, in high school I thought I would give youth group another try. But, yet again, I just didn't seem to fit in. I remember how much I loved playing group games. However, as You know, Lord, I have a hearing loss that caused me to miss some of the instructions. So, when it was time to play, I didn't know what to do. I would end up standing in the middle of the floor wondering why everyone was running around and what they were doing.

Still, I am grateful, Lord, that over and over You gave me the courage and strength to try again.

When the time came to try out the college ministry at my NEW church, I was understandably a little nervous. At first, I didn't know where I belonged or fit in. I walked into the room, and it seemed like everyone already had someone they were chatting with. I didn't know how to break in. And then, there was a turning point.

Now, I am part of a group with my peers where I truly belong. Perseverance pays off! Thank You, Lord, for giving me endurance.

In Jesus' name,
Amen.

YOUR TURN

Have you ever felt alone? Ignored? Abandoned? What did you do when you felt that way? Did someone reach out to you? Did you reach out to someone? Did you pray and ask God to guide you to the next step?

The next time you feel alone in a group, what will you do?

~~~~~~~~~~~~~~~~
~~~~~~~~~~~~~~~~

3

TRUST IN THE LORD

Dear Heavenly Father,

I'm still learning so much about You. Now, I am starting to want to spend time with my Heavenly Father 24/7!

I love You Lord! I trust You with my whole heart!

What is my passion? I want to renew my passion for You! What do You want me to do in life, Lord? Is it acting? Is it filmmaking? Is it writing mysteries and other kinds of stories?

I am having a hard time being patient as I figure out what you want me to do. I want to trust You. I am waiting for something to happen so badly. I know that I have to be okay with waiting. I do not want to lean on my own understanding. I want Your will.

Help me to keep trusting You.

In Jesus' name,
Amen!

YOUR TURN

What are things that you want to do that are not happening? Are you having trouble waiting for your prayers to be answered?

Make a list of some things that you wanted in the past that came true. Then, list as many good things as you can that are already in your life.

Now, make a list of things that you want to happen in the future.

Know that God's plans for you are perfect. Continue to pray and trust God for what He wants for you.

~~~~~~~~~~~~~~~
~~~~~~~~~~~~~~~

"But when I am afraid,
I will put my trust in You."
Psalm 56:3 (NLT)

4

FEAR NOT

Dear God,

So much has happened in my lifetime! Thank You for always being there for me.

Sometimes I struggle with fear. These things cause me to be afraid:

1. I am afraid I may unintentionally say hurtful or offensive things.

2. Because of my hearing loss, I can't really catch everything that is said. I often miss instructions for games or conversations, but I do not want to have to ask people to repeat themselves.

3. I am afraid people will not like me or that they will find me annoying.

4. I am afraid I may miss golden opportunities in acting, filmmaking, serving, education, and even friendships opportunities.

I don't want to be afraid of You or be so fearful of things. I know You are in control, and I want to keep trusting You, Lord!

In Jesus' name I pray,
Amen

YOUR TURN

What are you afraid of? How do you know that you can trust God?

Think about verses in the Bible that tell you why you know that you can trust God even when you're afraid.

<div align="center">~~~~~~~~~~~~~~~</div>

"For the wages of sin is death, but the gift of God is eternal life in Christ Jesus, our Lord."
Romans 6:23 (NIV)

5

THE GIFT OF GOD

I love You, Lord Jesus Christ!

Thank You for saving me. Help me to share the Gospel with people!

I do not want people to be separated from You forever, which is what happens when they are not saved. I want people to know that Jesus is our Savior, and that He came to earth as a person. He lived, died, was buried, and rose again to save sinners.

I know that we are all sinners and fall short of the glory of God. I know that sin brings death. I also know that Jesus paid the penalty for sin.

Thank You for what You are going to do!

In Jesus' name I pray,
Amen!

YOUR TURN

Are you saved? Do you know that Jesus died for your sins?
Have you received the gift of eternal life in Jesus?

No? You can ask Jesus to save you right now.
Yes? Then GO tell someone else.

~~~~~~~~~~~~~~~~

~~~~~~~~~~~~~~~~

"Your unfailing love, O Lord, is as vast as the heavens; Your
faithfulness reaches beyond the clouds.
Your righteousness is like the mighty mountains,
Your justice like the ocean depths.
You care for people and animals alike, O Lord."
Psalm 36:5-6 (NLT)

6

GOD CARES FOR YOU

Dear Lord Jesus,

Wow! I love how Your Word gives us descriptions of how very wide and deep and big YOU are, oh God. And yet . . .You care about me. You care about my family. You care about my friends. I am humbled to think that I am precious to You. I am grateful to know that You love me and that Your love is unfailing.

There is nothing in this world I love more than You, my Savior! Lord, I trust You. I need You. The world needs You. God, I believe with my whole heart that nothing is too hard for You! With You, my Lord, all things are possible!

Because of You, God, I am still here and alive even though I had such a difficult beginning and almost died several times when I was a baby. Because I **am** still here, sometimes I feel as if I must do something to make the world a better place. That can feel so overwhelming because the world is too big. But then I realize that nothing is too big for my God. The awesome God! Thank You, Jesus, for what You are going to do!

In Jesus' name I pray,
Amen

YOUR TURN

Let's take a Quiz:

How vast is God's unfailing love?
Where does God's faithfulness reach?
What is God's righteousness like?
What is God's justice like?

How does reading about God's care for you inspire you to find out what He has called you to do and to do it with all your heart?

~~~~~~~~~~~~~~~~
~~~~~~~~~~~~~~~~

7

THE RIGHT PATH

Lord,

Show me Your glory. Show me Your power. Show me the path You want me to take. Thank You for creating me. I love how You are not finished with me yet! What do You want me to do Lord?

You say that Your Word is a lamp and a light to guide me. You are taking me on a journey. So, let me be a student of Your Word. Help me spend time reading, meditating, and studying what You have to say in the Bible. Guide me to the passages that are perfect for my path right now.

Where do I go to find out what I am supposed to do next? Which path is the right path for me? Do You want me to do ministry? If so, what does that look like? Do I work on filmmaking? Do You want me to be a writer?

What I do know is this:
- ❖ I know You want me to love You, God, and love people. *Luke 10:27a*
- ❖ I know that You want me to tell others about Jesus. *Matthew 28:20*
- ❖ I know that You want me to rejoice always. *Philippians 4:4*
- ❖ I know that You want me to be joyful. *1 Thessalonians 5:16*
- ❖ I know that You want me to pray constantly. *1 Thessalonians 5:17*
- ❖ I know that You want me to be thankful. *1 Thessalonians 5:18*

In Jesus' name I pray,
Amen

YOUR TURN

Make a list of things that you know about God.

Now, make a list, like I did above, of the things you know that God wants you to do.

Next, pick one of those things you know that God wants you to do and make a plan of how you will accomplish that one thing.

For example, if I were to pick the one of mine that says: I know God wants me to "love God and love people," I could determine to do something to love a person. I could send a text or call someone on the telephone and tell them something I appreciate about them. Maybe, I could buy a special treat or gift for someone and mail it or take it to them. I could write a letter and mail it. Another thing I could do is serve at a food pantry or special dinner for Seniors. I could take time to video chat with my niece or build something with my nephew. There are so many ways to love people.

So, you make your list of things you know God wants you to do and then **DO ONE OF THEM!**

Make a note here of what you decide to do. Check back afterwards and jot some notes on how it went.

<div align="center">~~~~~~~~~~~~~~~</div>

"If a man has a hundred sheep and one of them wanders away, what will he do? Won't he leave the ninety-nine others on the hills and go out to search for the one that is lost?
And if he finds it, I tell you the truth, he will rejoice over it more than over the ninety-nine that didn't wander away!
In the same way, it is not my heavenly Father's will that even one of these little ones should perish."
Matthew 18:12-14 (NLT)

8

NEVER ALONE

God,

I don't want to be that lost sheep who wanders away! Help me to find my way to You! I want to hold Your hand! I feel safer that way.

Protect me, God, from evil and help me to get a good night's sleep. God, I know You are in control! I believe that with You, all things are possible!

I want to do the things I am called to do. Never do I want to be alone. Never do I want to be disconnected from You and be obsessed with idols.

Oh, Heavenly Father, thank You for loving me. I love You so much!

Thank You for helping me to never feel alone and left out.

In Your name I pray,
Amen

YOUR TURN

Have you ever felt alone or lost?

Say this out loud, "I am never alone."

Write your own prayer thanking God for never leaving you alone, even if you wander away.

~~~~~~~~~~~~~~~~
~~~~~~~~~~~~~~~~

"For God has not given us a spirit of fear and timidity, but of power, love, and self-discipline."
2 Timothy 1:7 (NLT)

9

BE BOLD AND BRAVE

Lord,

Thank You for how much You have used this verse in my life to help me know that fear does not come from You—power, love, and self-discipline do. As You know, this is one of my favorite verses. Please help me with my fears. Help me to keep realizing that You do not give me a spirit of fear, but You give me a spirit of love, power, and self-discipline. Thank You, God, that You are always with me. Help me to know what to say and do when I am with people.

What is my next step? I know the presentation that Mom, Dad, and I are giving soon is a *next step*, but I am afraid about saying the wrong thing when I get up to speak.

Father, when I am afraid, help me to be bold and brave! Help me to keep trusting You, Lord!

Lord, You are holy! I am trusting You with my whole life! Please help me, God, to act like the adult that I am! Like Paul, I want to give up my childish ways! I am learning a lot this year! More than ever! I love You God! I know You are in control! You've got this!

In Jesus' name I pray,
Amen

YOUR TURN

Draw a picture of yourself being brave, bold, and full of power.

Add to the picture a loving thing that you can do for someone else using that power.

<div align="center">~~~~~~~~~~~~~~~~</div>

10

Prayer

Lord,

There are things I am thinking about, but I don't know how to put them into words. God, only You know my thoughts before I think them. Where do You want me to be? Where do You want my parents to be? I am wondering how You will take care of all of our needs.

Lord, I don't like to beg but I'm begging You, please. Please pray for me and my parents. Show us Your glory! Show us Your power! God, I can't do this all on my own. I need You. I feel like something amazing is just around the corner, like a light at the end of the tunnel, but I am not there yet!

Jesus, You are the Light! Shine Your light at my feet and allow me to walk on the right path! God, You are awesome! (*1 John 1:5; Psalm 27:1; Psalm 119:105*)

I trust You Lord! Heavenly Father, please hear my prayers—desperate and joyful. I believe You can answer prayers. I believe no matter what, You are in control and will do great things! Holy, Holy, Holy, is the Lord God Almighty! (*Isaiah 41:10; Isaiah 6:3; Revelation 4:8*)

Thank You, Jesus for what You are going to do! I love You, Father!

In Jesus' name I pray,
Amen

Do you have trouble figuring out how to pray or what words to say?

One thing you can do is to pray using the words in the Bible. For example, pick a prayer passage and make it personal.

~~~~~~~~~~~~~~~~

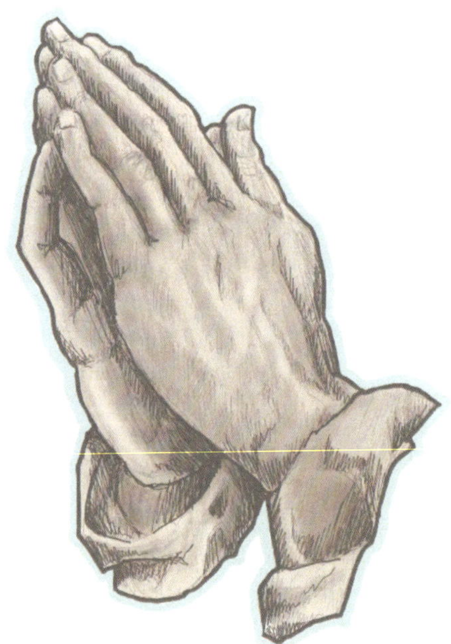
~~~~~~~~~~~~~~~~

11

PLEASING GOD

Dear God,

Please give me the desire and the power to do what pleases You. Thank You for working in me. There are so many things I like to do that I have always wanted to do, but now I just want to have the desire to do what YOU have planned for me to do.

How do You want me to do what pleases You? What does that look like? Who should that involve? Where is the best place to serve? When is the best time?

Let me always come back to the big WHY. The big why is: What will please You?

I want to do YOUR will, not mine!

Savior Jesus Christ, thank You for saving me.

I'm sorry, Lord, if I ever disobey You even when I don't know it. I love You, God! You are awesome! I pray others will see Your great works! I cannot wait to see You, Lord!

In Jesus' name,
Amen

YOUR TURN

How do you feel knowing that God is working in you?

Ask a trusted family member or friend what they see in you that shows you have a desire and the power to do what pleases God.

~~~~~~~~~~~~~~~~
~~~~~~~~~~~~~~~~

"Jesus looked at them and said, 'With man this is impossible,
but with God all things are possible.'"
Matthew 19:26 (NIV)

12

NOTHING IS IMPOSSIBLE

Dear Lord,

Here I am again thinking about possibilities. I feel happier when I make videos, do some acting, do public speaking, and hang out with friends and family.

God, I also feel better about life when I pray, listen to Christian music, write to You, and read Your Word, the Bible.

God, You are amazing!

What are Your plans for me? Father, I don't want to be stuck and focus too much on things that are not in front of me.

Lord, I don't know which way You are taking me, but I DO know that Jesus is the Way, the Truth, and the Life!

You've got this, God! I need You. All things are possible with You!

In Jesus' name,
Amen

YOUR TURN

Get quiet for a minute and think about something that God has done that is recorded in the Bible that seemed totally impossible, but that God made happen.

Focusing on God's power gives us confidence to know Him better and to trust Him.

~~~~~~~~~~~~~~~~
~~~~~~~~~~~~~~~~

"For I can do everything through Christ, who gives me strength." Philippians 4:13 (NLT)

"For I know the plans I have for you," says the LORD. "They are plans for good and not for disaster, to give you a future and a hope." Jeremiah 29:11 (NLT)

13

$\mathcal{H}$OPE FOR THE FUTURE

God, You are awesome!

My parents are encouraging me to do the things that You put right in front of me. Right now, I know You want me to audition to do drama for Vacation Bible School like I did last year.

I know You want me to take care of the body You have given me. I know You want me to be in Your Word, the Bible, every day. I know that You want me to talk to You (pray) every day.

I know that You want me to reach out in some way every day to others. I know that You want me to serve in Your community in some way. I know that You want me to love You.

Lord, I love You with all my heart. I am not sure exactly what doors You will open for me, but I do know that You have plans to give me hope and a future. You are my Heavenly Father!

Thank You, Jesus, for Your amazing works. I love You and will love You forever and ever!

In Your name I pray,
Amen

YOUR TURN

One person we know in the Bible who probably got discouraged and may have had trouble believing that God had a future and a hope for him is Joseph (*Genesis 37-50*).

Do a role play. Pretend that you are Joseph and ask someone you know to pretend to be Joseph's friend. You, as Joseph, are telling this friend one by one all the hard things that happened to you. The friend's job is to keep reminding you how God used that particular circumstance for your good.

Switch roles and do it again.

~~~~~~~~~~~~~~~~
~~~~~~~~~~~~~~~~

"No, dear brothers and sisters, I have not achieved it, but I focus on this one thing: Forgetting the past and looking forward to what lies ahead, I press on to reach the end of the race and receive the heavenly prize for which God, through Christ Jesus, is calling us."
Philippians 3:13,14 (NLT)

14

PRESSING ON

God,

Help me to look forward and not dwell on the past. The past is over. However, the future has not happened, and I do not want to waste my future by wishing to change the past. Lord, You know how much I struggle with this past thinking. Happy memories are awesome, but only if I don't spend all my todays and tomorrows thinking about the past.

For example, I have such happy memories from family times at the beach, and I want to go again. Now, it is time to make new memories. I can still go to the beach, but it won't be the same as before—it will be new. It will be better!

No matter what, it is good to know that YOU never change. You are always present. You are calling my heart right now for now.

I am praying and giving my thoughts to You. All things are possible with You, God! Nothing is too hard for You! I'm trusting You, Lord! Use me in a way I can never imagine, for Your glory! I love You, Lord Jesus! Where do You want me to go? What can I do to serve You? How can I serve?

Thank You for what You are going to do!

In Jesus' name,
Amen

YOUR TURN

Take several sheets of 8 ½ x 11 paper, fold the stack in half, then number the pages.

In the first third of the book draw pictures, write short descriptions or paste in photos or pics of things that remind you of happy times in your past.

In the middle third of the book show some things that describe your life right now.

In the last third of the book show—by drawing, pasting, or writing—what dreams you have for the future.

~~~~~~~~~~~~~~~~
~~~~~~~~~~~~~~~~

"The faithful love of the LORD never ends! His mercies never cease.
Great is His faithfulness; His mercies begin afresh each morning."
Lamentations 3:22-23 (NLT)

15

UNENDING MERCY

Lord,

I know that Your mercies never end.

I need mercy because I deserve death. I am a sinner and am separated from You, God, without Jesus.

Thank You that Your faithfulness and love never end.

Without Jesus, I am lost and afraid. I need You, God.

I need Your compassion, mercy, faithfulness, and love.

Jesus, thank You for saving me! You are not finished with me yet!

I am excited to see You working in my life! I want to be ready and not worry too much!

In Jesus' name,
Amen

YOUR TURN

Do you ever feel like you have "blown it?" Do you sometimes think that you have royally messed up?

You are not alone. We all feel that way at some time or another. What is comforting to know is this: God's mercies are new every morning. No matter how tough the day before was, God's faithful love never ends.

Know that you can stop and ask God to forgive you and that His mercies never cease. He is ready to forgive you. He is ready to give you a NEW mercy. You can wake up refreshed and rejoice over a new day with new mercies.

On a nice day, go outside with a piece of sidewalk chalk. Draw a flower with a big bloom. Look at that flower as a symbol of God's new mercies.

~~~~~~~~~~~~~~~

~~~~~~~~~~~~~~~

"People who conceal their sins will not prosper, but if they confess and turn from them, they will receive mercy." Proverbs 28:13 (NLT)

16

CONFESSION

Dear God,

Please forgive me for the sins I am confessing to You. I need Your mercy.

You know I just finished doing a Bible study about putting other gods before You. I think my gods in the past have been computer games, tv shows, and message boards.

I found myself using these things to fill a hole in my heart that should have been filled by You. I know now that You fill this hole with Your Word, communication with You through prayer, worship music, and godly relationships.

I know I am not perfect. I know I am a sinner. Thank You for loving me. Heavenly Father, I love You more than anything. You are awesome, and I thank You for Your amazing grace and forgiveness!

In Jesus' name I pray,
Amen

YOUR TURN

Is there a sin that you need to turn away from? Is there anything you need to confess to God? Is there something that you would rather do than pray?

Do you know Jesus as your Savior? Take a minute right now and ask God to fill the hole inside of you with Jesus and ask Him to forgive your sins.

Put Jesus first in all that you do.

~~~~~~~~~~~~~~~
~~~~~~~~~~~~~~~

"For this is how God loved the world: He gave His one and only Son, so that everyone who believes in Him will not perish but have eternal life.
God sent His Son into the world not to judge the world, but to save the world through Him."
John 3:16-17 (NLT)

17

LIFE ETERNAL

Dear Lord,

Thank You for sending Your only begotten Son so that I can have eternal life. I have dreams about things I would like to be and do, but I want my dreams to line up with sharing that Jesus saves, which is the Gospel message.

What will show Your glory best? Sometimes I just love to sit and think about the possibilities:

For writing, I could write devotionals. For acting, I could be in a Christian film or television series, family friendly television entertainment, or maybe something totally new that I haven't thought of where I can show people how awesome You are!

God, You are AWESOME! So mighty to save! Thanks for giving me JOY!

Thank You for what You are going to do!

In Jesus' name,
Amen!

YOUR TURN

Do you have eternal life? Have you asked Jesus to be your Savior?

 If you have, create something that will remind you about it. For example, my mom knows that she asked Jesus into her heart in September when she was 19 years old. She wrote that date in her Bible at the time.

You can paint a rock with a date and/or a verse to remind you.

You can make a bookmark with a reminder on it. Get creative.

~~~~~~~~~~~~~~~~
~~~~~~~~~~~~~~~~

18

DELIGHT IN THE LORD

Lord,

You are enough! Help me to be fully satisfied in YOU. I do delight in You, Lord. I delight in that You kept me alive when I was a baby. I almost died, but You wanted me to live and grow up with my brother, sisters, mom, and dad.

You gave me the ability to see, hear, walk, talk, think, learn, and grow.

I want to live for You! I want to bring You glory. I want to help others grow in Christ.

Thank You for giving me the ability to make videos, write, speak publicly, work in ministry, serve at church, and much more.

Thank You for my family!

I want my desires to be Your desires. I want to be Your instrument. I want to be Your vessel. I want You to work through me to do Your work.

Thank You, Jesus, for what You are going to do!

In Your name I pray,
Amen

YOUR TURN

Can you think of 5 ways in which you can take delight in the Lord?

Maybe you can take delight in nature—watch a bunny rabbit hop across your yard or take note of the intricate flight of a bird overhead.

Maybe you can take delight in the Lord by recognizing someone's ability or kindness.

You can take delight in the Lord by getting still and praying to Him and listening with your heart.

What else can you do to take delight in the Lord?

<div align="center">~~~~~~~~~~~~~~</div>

"We can make our plans,
but the LORD determines our steps."
Proverbs 16:9 (NLT)

19

Perfect Plans

Dear God,

My mind is going and going. I don't know where it's going or how to stop dreaming . . .

God, I don't want to miss a thing You have in store for me!

I have had so many dreams and ideas but don't know where to start.

Help me to believe and trust in Your perfect timing!

I want to be patient. More patient.

Waiting is so hard, but, Lord, I believe what You have planned will be worth the wait.

Thank You for what You are going to do!

In Jesus' Name,
Amen

Draw a picture of a staircase. Picture God holding your hand as you take each step.

Think about the plans you are making for yourself. Do you think they are in line with what God teaches us in His Word?

If not, pray for God to redirect you.

If so, ask God to tweak your plans according to what He wants for you.

Post your picture of the staircase somewhere you can see it and be reminded that God is determining your steps.

~~~~~~~~~~~~~~~~
~~~~~~~~~~~~~~~~

"But the Holy Spirit produces this kind of fruit in our lives: love, joy, peace, patience, kindness, goodness, faithfulness, gentleness, and self-control. There is no law against these things!"
Galatians 5:22-23 (NLT)

20

$\mathcal{B}$EARING FRUIT

Dear Heavenly Father,

Love: Thank You for loving me even though I am a sinner. Now, help me to love others the way You love me.

Joy: Thank You for giving me joy! Help me to spread Your joy all around.

Peace: I love knowing that there is nothing to worry about because You are in control! Help me to keep trusting You. Help me to also share this message of peace with others.

Patience: It is so hard to be patient. I am grateful to have Your help because I know that I cannot be patient without it. Help me to be patient with Your will and with other people.

You give the fruit of the Spirit, and You work it in me. There is nothing my God cannot do!

Lord, You're so awesome! Thank You for keeping me alive! I am excited to go to Heaven and see You, but I'm also excited about Your plans for me here on Earth.

I pray, Lord, that I would meet new neighbors and become the "God's Girl" You had in mind since the very beginning of the universe! You know the plans, and You are writing my life story! I love You, Heavenly Father! Use me in a way I could never imagine!

In Jesus' name,
Amen

Gather together some beads, or something you can use as symbols, and a length of string. This project is to find a bead or symbol that represents each of the fruit of the Holy Spirit named in this verse.

You can use different colored beads. For example, a red bead for love, a white bead for peace, a blue bead for joy, etc.

You could also use shapes for symbols of the different fruit. For example, you can use a heart to represent love, a dove to represent peace, etc.

Keep this as a reminder of the fruit of the Holy Spirit that you have available within you if you are a child of God.

~~~~~~~~~~~~~~~~

~~~~~~~~~~~~~~~~

"Rejoice always, pray continually, give thanks in all circumstances; for this is God's will for you in Christ Jesus."
1 Thessalonians 5:16-18 (NIV)

21

A THANKFUL HEART

Lord,

Sometimes I am not grateful. Sometimes I am not thankful. My dad is so wonderful to share this verse with me so that I can think the right way.

There are times when I am not being thankful. When we lived in the country house, I was unhappy and not thankful because everything was so far away, and we had very little internet. These things were important to me—more important than trusting Your plan for me. I am sorry, God.

I was sad and not rejoicing or being thankful when I did not get a part I wanted in a play. Sometimes I get stuck thinking too much about the past. For example, I wonder if life would be better if I had made different choices or different decisions in the past?

When I remember this verse, I realize that You know everything. You do everything for Your glory and my good. Thank You for giving me a great life!

I know I'm not perfect, but You are. I don't like doing wrong things, and I do want to keep on praying, rejoicing always, and giving thanks in all circumstances!

Thank You for Your Word!

In Jesus' name I pray,
Amen

If you are a child of God, you will want to please Him—you will want to do His will.

Let's try another Quiz.
What three things is Paul saying in this verse to the Thessalonians and to us that are the will of God?

1.

2.

3.

Now think about specific ways that you can do all three.

~~~~~~~~~~~~~~~~
~~~~~~~~~~~~~~~~

22

 SEEK AND FIND

Lord,

I want to see You!

I want to get to know Your will!

Your will be done!

I just want to keep trusting and believing that You are with me always.

Never will I ever want to give up.

Thank You for what You are going to do!

I love You, Lord!

Help me to know what to say and do!

In Jesus' name I pray,
Amen

YOUR TURN

There are SO many verses in the Bible that talk about seeking God and the results you will receive when you do.

For this activity you will need your Bible, a notepad, and a prominent place that you see all the time where you can stick the notes.

Do a Bible search for the word "seek." Write each verse on a different note page.

Here are a few references to get you started: *Jeremiah 29:13, 2 Chronicles 15:2b, Matthew 7:7.*

~~~~~~~~~~~~~~~~
~~~~~~~~~~~~~~~~

23

GOD IS IN CONTROL

Lord,

I thank You for Your words in my heart.

Never do I ever want to worry about what's happening tomorrow.

I believe You've got this under control!

Help me to keep going on the right path.

I can't wait to see what You have planned for my life and the lives of my family and friends.

You are an amazing God!

In Jesus' Name,
Amen

Here is a demonstration that you can do to teach someone about putting God first. If we learn to seek God and put Him first, our worries will lessen, and our peace will increase.

<u>PREP</u>: So, you need these supplies: 1) a rock, 2) some rice, 3) a container with a lid. You will want to use a rock that is large enough to take up most of the room of the container but not all of it. Put the rock in the container and then put enough rice in to fill the container. Now take out the rock and set it aside. Take out the rice and put it in a bowl.

<u>GO TIME</u>: Start the demonstration by identifying that the rock represents God and the rice represents everything else in life (family, friends, possessions, activities, job, etc.) that we tend to focus on instead of or more than God. Put the rock in the container while stating that we always want God to be first in our life.

Then, take the rice and fill in the rest of the space while stating that first God should take up most of the space of your life and then you can fill your life with the rest. Put the lid on the container to show how everything fits well.

Next, do the opposite. Put the rice in first and try to fit the rock in around the rice. Try to put the lid on. You will see that the rice does not fit if the rock is not in the container first.

LESSON: If God is not first in your life, all the rest of life does not fit well.

~~~~~~~~~~~~~~~~
~~~~~~~~~~~~~~~~

*"I pray that God, the source of hope, will fill you completely
with joy and peace because you trust in Him.
Then you will overflow with confident hope through the power of
the Holy Spirit."*
Romans 15:13 (NLT)

24

OUR SOURCE OF HOPE

Dear God,

Thank You for being my source of hope and always giving me that hope even when I am having a hard day!

I can be completely filled with joy and peace no matter what!

I want to keep on trusting You, Lord!

Without You, I wouldn't have hope, joy, or peace.

But with You in my heart, I can have confident hope because it comes from YOU!

I love You, Lord Jesus!

In Your name,
Amen

Friend, are you discouraged today? Are you without hope? Then, I pray this prayer for you.

I pray that God, the source of hope, will fill you completely with joy and peace BECAUSE you trust Him.

You can, you know—trust Him. He loves you so much. He made you—fearfully and wonderfully. You are precious to Him.

Take that step and trust Him. Lean into His promises. Let the Holy Spirit fill you with His power.

~~~~~~~~~~~~~~~
~~~~~~~~~~~~~~~

"This is My command—be strong and courageous!
Do not be afraid or discouraged.
For the LORD your God is with you wherever you go."
Joshua 1:9 (NLT)

25

BE STRONG AND COURAGEOUS

God,

I know You want me to be strong and courageous. Sometimes I do not feel strong or full of courage. When people ask me questions that I cannot answer, I am afraid that I will say the wrong thing.

Sometimes, I do not feel strong enough, physically. I also do not feel strong when I struggle with expressing my thoughts or feelings accurately. When I feel left out, I feel lost and scared and do not know where to turn sometimes. I do not feel courageous.

When I am feeling convicted in Bible study, sometimes I just well up with tears. I just want to run away. I do not feel strong. I do not have courage to stay. I am afraid I will not know how to explain why I am emotional.

That is why this verse helps me. I need to know that the Lord is with me wherever I go. Thank You for that truth, that mercy, that grace and that love.

I pray, Lord, that I can be bold and brave and that I'm not afraid to do anything You call me to do. I love that You are with me always—that I'm not alone! Help me to be more aware of You and Your truth in life. Thank You, Lord for being with me!

In Jesus' name,
Amen

YOUR TURN

Find a small pebble that can easily be slipped into your pocket.

Paint the words "strong" or "courageous" or both "strong & courageous" on the stone in a bright color.

Keep the stone handy and available to put into your pocket on those days that you are feeling particularly weak or discouraged. Slip your hand into your pocket and rub the stone to remind you of God's promises—that He will be with you wherever you go!

~~~~~~~~~~~~~~~

~~~~~~~~~~~~~~~

*"For the LORD your God is living among you.
He is a mighty savior. He will take delight in you with
gladness. With His love, He will calm all your fears.
He will rejoice over you with joyful songs."*
Zephaniah 3:17 (NLT)

26

HE DELIGHTS IN YOU

Dear God,

This verse reminds me of the song *Mighty to Save* by Hillsong.

The song talks about how no matter what life gives me or if I'm feeling alone or scared . . .

You always provide, protect, and prevail.

I love that You will calm all my fears with Your love.

You rejoice whenever I sing worship songs!

Thank You, Lord, for giving me a mighty Savior!

In Jesus' name I pray,
Amen

YOUR TURN

Sidewalk Chalk Time!

Go outside with a piece of sidewalk chalk and draw a great big happy face.

Take a picture of it.

Save this picture and look at it whenever you want to remember that God takes delight in you with gladness.

~~~~~~~~~~~~~~~~
~~~~~~~~~~~~~~~~

"Therefore, go and make disciples of all the nations, baptizing them in the name of the Father and the Son and the Holy Spirit. Teach these new disciples to obey all the commands I have given you. And be sure of this: I am with you always, even to the end of the age."'
Matthew 28:19-20 (NLT)

27

 SHARE WITH OTHERS

Dear Lord Jesus,

I pray that I am able to tell people about You.

I know I had a rough start when I was born.

Thank You for keeping me alive, God!

There must be a reason why I am reading this passage.

Help me to reach out more and keep Your commandments!

In Jesus' name I pray,
Amen

How do we make disciples? Here are some ideas:

❖ Prayerfully consider who you might tell about Jesus this week. Share the gospel message that Jesus lived, suffered, died, and rose again to save us from our sins.

❖ Do Bible study with a new believer so that they know the God who made them and saved them and who walks with them every day. Teach them how to obey the things in God's Word.

❖ Be a good example of what it means to be a Christ-follower.

~~~~~~~~~~~~~~~
~~~~~~~~~~~~~~~

28

HE HEARS US

Lord,

I pray that I can keep being confident that You hear me when I call!

Thank You for what You have done in my life.

I don't always know what You want me to do, but I believe in You and trust Your perfect timing!

Help me to pray for what pleases You.

In Jesus' name I pray,
Amen

In this verse, John tells us when we can be confident that God hears us.

What is the condition?

Ponder what you think you can ask for that would please Him.

~~~~~~~~~~~~~~~
~~~~~~~~~~~~~~~

*"Don't let anyone think less of you because you are young.
Be an example to all believers in what you say, in the way you
live, in your love, your faith, and your purity."
1 Timothy 4:12 (NLT)*

29

CHILD OF THE KING

Dear God,

I love that no matter how old or young I am, I can still praise You and tell others about You!

Jesus once said all children come to Him—we are all Your children and I'm happy to be a daughter to a King!

Thank You, Lord, for accepting me as Your child.

I know that I am protected by Your loving arms. Thank You!

In Jesus' name I pray,
Amen

YOUR TURN

David knew what it was like to be thought less of because of his age. He was young—the youngest of eight brothers.

He found out when he took his brothers a meal that the Israelites were afraid of the army of the Philistines and especially Goliath, a giant of a man who was part of the Philistine army. David was young. David was misunderstood. Yet, he knew that the Israelites were God's people.

He knew that God would give him what he needed to stop the giant. Refresh your memory by reading 1 Samuel 17 and then tell someone the story.

~~~~~~~~~~~~~~~

</div>
~~~~~~~~~~~~~~~

30

A JOYFUL NOISE

God,

While I may not be the world's most perfect singer, I love to sing praise songs! Thank You for those who pick the songs at church—the singers and the writers of the songs are amazing! When I am afraid, nervous, joyful, or just don't know what to do, I sing or listen to worship songs!

Worship songs remind me of who You are, God.

For example, *Follow You Anywhere* sung by Passion, is one of my favorites. This song helps me to know that all I need is Jesus.

This is Amazing Grace sung by Phil Wickham helps me to remember all that Jesus did for me by taking my place on the cross. He died for my sins. And . . . He is King of all. Thank You, Jesus.

Open up the Heavens by Meredith Andrews points my eyes and heart to You. I love singing, "Show us, show us Your glory, show us, show us Your power, show us, show us Your glory, Lord!"

Thank You for letting me sing a joyful noise to You, God!

In Jesus' name I pray,
Amen

It is time to worship with singing.

Pick two or three worship songs that you love and sing them out to the Lord!

~~~~~~~~~~~~~~~~
~~~~~~~~~~~~~~~~

"So whether you eat or drink, or whatever you do,
do it all for the glory of God."
1 Corinthians 10:31(NLT)

31

GLORY OF GOD

God,

Anything I do, I want to do it all for Your glory.

- ❖ When I make videos, I want to make them for Your glory.

- ❖ When I write, I want to write for Your glory.

- ❖ When I serve at the Welcome Desk at my church, I want to serve for Your glory.

- ❖ When I act with the VBS drama team or with the Virginia Christmas Spectacular, I want to act for Your glory.

- ❖ When I do my chores, I want to work with a good attitude and for Your glory.

- ❖ When I exercise and take care of my body by eating healthy foods, I want to be healthy for Your glory.

- ❖ When I listen to music, I want to choose music that honors You—for Your glory.

Help me to focus on the message in the videos I make to encourage others in their walk with You. Help me to write things that draw people to You. Help me to be friendly and confident in answering questions at the Welcome Desk so that I can represent You well. Help me to be upbeat, entertaining, and to give a good message when I act.

Thank You, Lord for Your glory! Keep showing Your glory through me!

In Jesus' name I pray,
Amen

Write a personal prayer like the one above.

Start with: "When I ______________ [*fill in the blank with something you do*], I want to do it for Your glory."

Write at least four more and finish it by asking God to help you to do all things for His glory.

~~~~~~~~~~~~~~~~~
~~~~~~~~~~~~~~~~~

*"I know the LORD is always with me.
I will not be shaken, for He is right beside me."*
Psalm 16:8 (NLT)

32

BESIDE ME ALWAYS

Dear God,

Thank You for being beside me always. I do not need to be afraid:

- ❖ when I am discouraged about dreams that haven't come true yet,

- ❖ when people ask me questions and I do not know the answers or I do not know how to accurately answer them or express my thoughts,

- ❖ when people do not understand how to interact with me,

- ❖ when people think that I am a child and treat me like one,

because You are here in my heart!

I love You, Lord!

I need You always!

In Jesus' name I pray,
Amen

YOUR TURN

If you like to draw, sketch a picture of the back of someone with an arm around their shoulder.

Now close your eyes and picture that God has His arm around your shoulder.

Thank Him that He is always with you—even closer than a friend!

~~~~~~~~~~~~~~~~
~~~~~~~~~~~~~~~~

33

SETTING PRIORITIES

Dear Lord Jesus,

Thank You for showing me the things I made idols or false gods. An idol is something worshipped that is not YOU—the one true God.

I had no idea that I had idols. Thank You for leading me to participate in that women's Bible study where I learned about the sin of obsessing on anything but You. I looked at my life and saw that I did have idols.

My idols, as You know, were things like kids and teens programs on television, a Christian singing group, and computer games. All of these choices were not bad ones. They did not have bad language. They did not have sinful overtones like drugs, excessive alcohol, sexual sins, etc. So, I thought they were okay. However, they did have the ability to draw me in and capture me.

Thank You for showing me that anything that captures me more than You is sinful. Thank You for forgiving my sins and please protect me from evil. While the things I was into were not bad and some were even good, I was into them too much. Help me to let go of the past and move on.

Thank You, Heavenly Father for what You are going to do!

In Jesus' name I pray,
Amen

What are your idols? Are you worshipping something more than God?

How are you spending your time? A good activity to find that out is to track your time.

Create a document with 15 minute or half hour increments. Periodically throughout your day, record how you are spending your time. What is your recreation? Is there time each day for personal prayer and worship time with your Lord? Do you study His Word?

~~~~~~~~~~~~~~~
~~~~~~~~~~~~~~~

"So let's not get tired of doing what is good.
At just the right time we will reap a harvest of blessing if we
don't give up."
Galatians 6:9 (NLT)

34

NEVER GIVE UP

Dear God,

Thank You for giving me a harvest of blessing when I don't give up.

I may be tired and at times I want to quit, but with Your help, I won't give up!

Thank You for what You are going to do, Lord Jesus!

Help me to keep on trusting You and be patient for Your perfect timing for that harvest of blessing!

Let me be able to always see the blessings that You send.

In Jesus' name I pray,
Amen

YOUR TURN

Never give up. God wants us to persevere. It is hard to keep pressing on when things are difficult.

But always remember this—God is with you. He is ready to give you everything you need for life and godliness. Learn to lean on Him.

Get some modeling clay that hardens. Fashion the clay into something that looks like a medal. You may want to etch the reference of this verse or another verse that reminds you to never quit into the surface of your medal. Now you have a reminder. You may even want to make medals like this for others to help them remember.

~~~~~~~~~~~~~~~~
~~~~~~~~~~~~~~~~

"The LORD is my light and my salvation—so why should I be afraid?
The LORD is my fortress, protecting me from danger, so why should I tremble?"
Psalm 27:1-2 (NLT)

35

TRUST GOD WHEN AFRAID

Dear Heavenly Father,

Please help me to know that you are the Light.

You are my salvation. That is all I need.

I am trusting You, God, with my whole heart.

I need You, Lord! I can't do anything on my own!

Thank you for inspiring Chris Tomlin to sing the song, *Whom Shall I Fear (God of Angel Armies)*. It is a great inspiration to me.

In Jesus' name I pray,
Amen

Here are two activities that you can do to remind you of these verses:
1. Light a candle and watch it flicker while reciting the verse over and over until you have it memorized.
2. Find materials that you can use to build a "fortress." Invite some friends and build a fortress with building blocks or blankets and pillows. Use craft material of various types (i.e. marshmallows and toothpicks, cardboard boxes, etc.) to create a fortress.

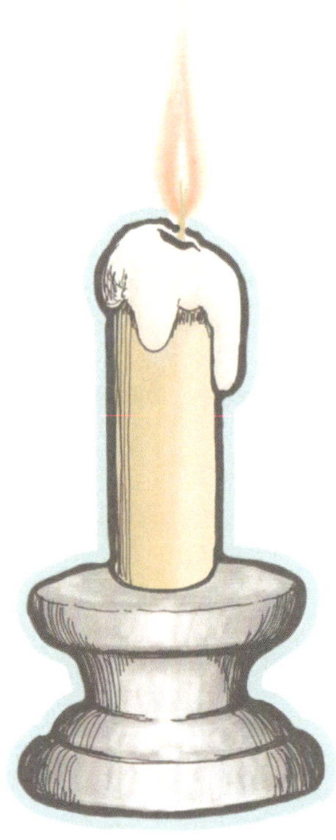

~~~~~~~~~~~~~~~~
~~~~~~~~~~~~~~~~

Amy's Story

My mom went into labor with me one month early. I was born not breathing, and the nurses and doctors rushed me away to the NICU, the Neonatal Intensive Care Unit.

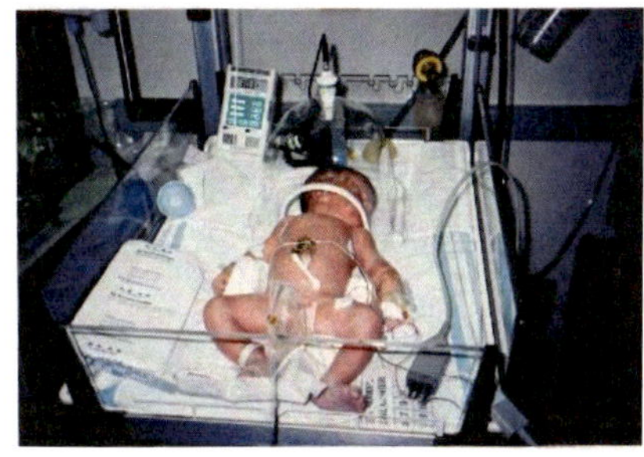

When I was two days old, a geneticist from a big teaching hospital came to our small hospital and diagnosed me with CHARGE Syndrome.

After two weeks, the NICU released me to go home to my family. A few days before my discharge, the NICU doctor told my mom that I most likely would be blind, deaf, and mentally challenged. She said that I probably would not be able to walk, talk, or eat by mouth. Those early days were very uncertain. I was a sick little baby.

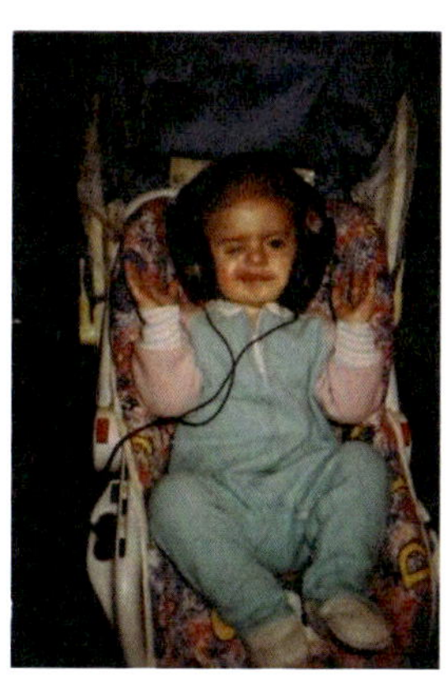

But God. He decided that I should live and that I should do more than the prognosis. I am so very grateful.

As I grew, all I knew was that I wanted to keep up with my three older siblings.

My parents decided to work extra hard with me to stimulate my brain to open new pathways and make new connections which, in turn, gave me more abilities.

My growing abilities surprised everyone and exceeded everyone's expectations.

While I still have disabilities, I have way more abilities than anyone could have imagined. I struggle with a pretty significant hearing loss, which can be frustrating sometimes. However, I walk well. I do public speaking, and since I was 20 years old, I have been eating 100% by mouth. My mind keeps going and going and going. I love technology and working with the ministry.

I look forward to more journaling and learning more about photography, videography, and traveling.

To find more about Amy

Visit us on our website: Champions4Parents.com
Follow us on Facebook: Champions4Parents

Visit Amy on her website at HeartReCHARGE.com

Follow Amy on Facebook: Amy's Story, God's Glory
Follow Amy on Instagram: Amy's Story, God's Glory
Subscribe to Amy's YouTube channel: amycvideos
Follow Amy on Twitter: @AmyChristine412

Email Amy at champions4parents@gmail.com